A Poem For Some Days

Camille Excell

BookLeaf Publishing

India | USA | UK

Presentation by *BookLeaf Publishing*

Web: www.bookleafpub.com

E-mail: info@bookleafpub.com

ISBN: 9789357448499

First edition 2022

DEDICATION

For Morgy,

thanks.

ACKNOWLEDGEMENT

I would like to acknowledge the traditional owners of this land upon which we read, create and stand: The Wurundjeri people of the Kulin Nation, and pay my respects to elders past, present and future. I acknowledge that sovereignty has never been ceded.

The colour spectrum

Today was grey;
      there was something a-drift.
Heavy, but almost like spring.

Rehearsal

Technique is the water and I am the wave.
Tomorrow, I'll do it.
But today I'm afraid.

Getting up early

Creating fire in the belly
can come at a price.
Sometimes you must turn off the heat
and refreeze the ice.

Optus

I keep dreaming dreams,
where I am in trouble-
my phone will not work.

My fingers are giant,
the buttons minuscule,
the speaker is broken,
and there's no one to call.

Winter

I can't feel it yet
your full extent.

My teeth ache for the smiles
that once bled from your cheeks.

And now you're dark circles, long stares,
confused at the cold.
You thought that winter had passed, a long while
ago.

In the mirror, I found you

I looked like you
with the blood shot eyes
and the dandruff.

From the side,
in that picture.

When I showered,
and combed my hair slick.

I looked like you
when you smiled
and I twinkled back.

On campus

I walk around the lake
      just to be inspired.

I cultivate hate
(for you)
      just to be inspired.

I have a glass of wine
      and pretend that I am normal
Then I sleep for sixteen hours
      with the hope that as time passes

I will be inspired.

Wives and Daughters (Elizabeth Gaskell)

Not sure how,
but I heard somebody say
that you had a death wish,
tucked away,
in the drawers with the pearls.

Acoustic

I got the brains,
she got the money.
My mothers lips
were sweeter than honey.

They dripped warmly
from a wooden spoon
until the sky iced over
and blacked out the moon.

Modesty

Mother's on a sinking ship,
she's tossing out the sails.
She's plucking out her bright blue eyes
and screaming to the whales.

The waves, they ravage
and the ship continues sinking.
So Mother, then, cuts out her tongue
and God continues drinking.

Vignettes

A. I loved playing in the dirt,
and then I loved to get clean again

…

B. Our ancestors were here
but luckily, they dried up.
Before we became machines.

….

C. Your head was round and it bled,
profusely.
Until your soul came out.

…

D. I slid down your golden hair,
until I couldn't slide anymore.
I wore a beetle suit and still,
you ignored me.

…

E. Keep going,
Keep glueing,
until you have erased your mistakes.

Murder Mystery

The housewife?
She's unhappy
and tries to
POISON
her children.

Then I thought she had killed her self!
But it was just tomato sauce.

Ouch

That's where it hurt;
in my 'not just a body'.

But a soundboard, a siphon, a funnel, a t i p, a
DARTboard, a wasteland, agraceland, a H E L L
, a childhood home, a mortuary, adoppleganger
adoppleganger, a b o x of s e c r e t s, a bird,
a
human
woman.

Midnight

I spill my wine
through the air
in front of my face,
and it drips,
cracking the glassware
shattering the window pane.

And inside, sits Aphrodite.
Finally free
to take the plunge.

Nightmare

I tell myself, as if I'm the queen
that 'I can do it without them.'
Then I remember I've had five glasses of wine,
100 sushi rolls, three doughnuts, 10 joints, 1000
litres of diet coke,
and one reoccurring dream.

The roof is leaking

I saw it smash, shatter
    in slow motion.
I thought that, despite the cracks,
the hot liquid that ran and stang
    when I reached for the pieces
that we would remain intact,
    still and despite
    our tears.

Circus school

Fundamentally,
          you're walking a tightrope.
Between us, between the two.

Wildlife, she screams below you
and above you dangle.
You dangle, and you bite.

Crack

You meet me in the middle of my back
            Crack.
Our fingers pull
and pop like kernels
burning and expiring in liquid flame.

Tiny paper cranes are crammed
into my iris my corneas
and if they could speak
they would be screaming.

Sitdi

You're beautiful, strong.
Perfumed water rolls perfectly
down the bridge of your nose,
pooling in an inkwell
in which you dip
you quill
to write.